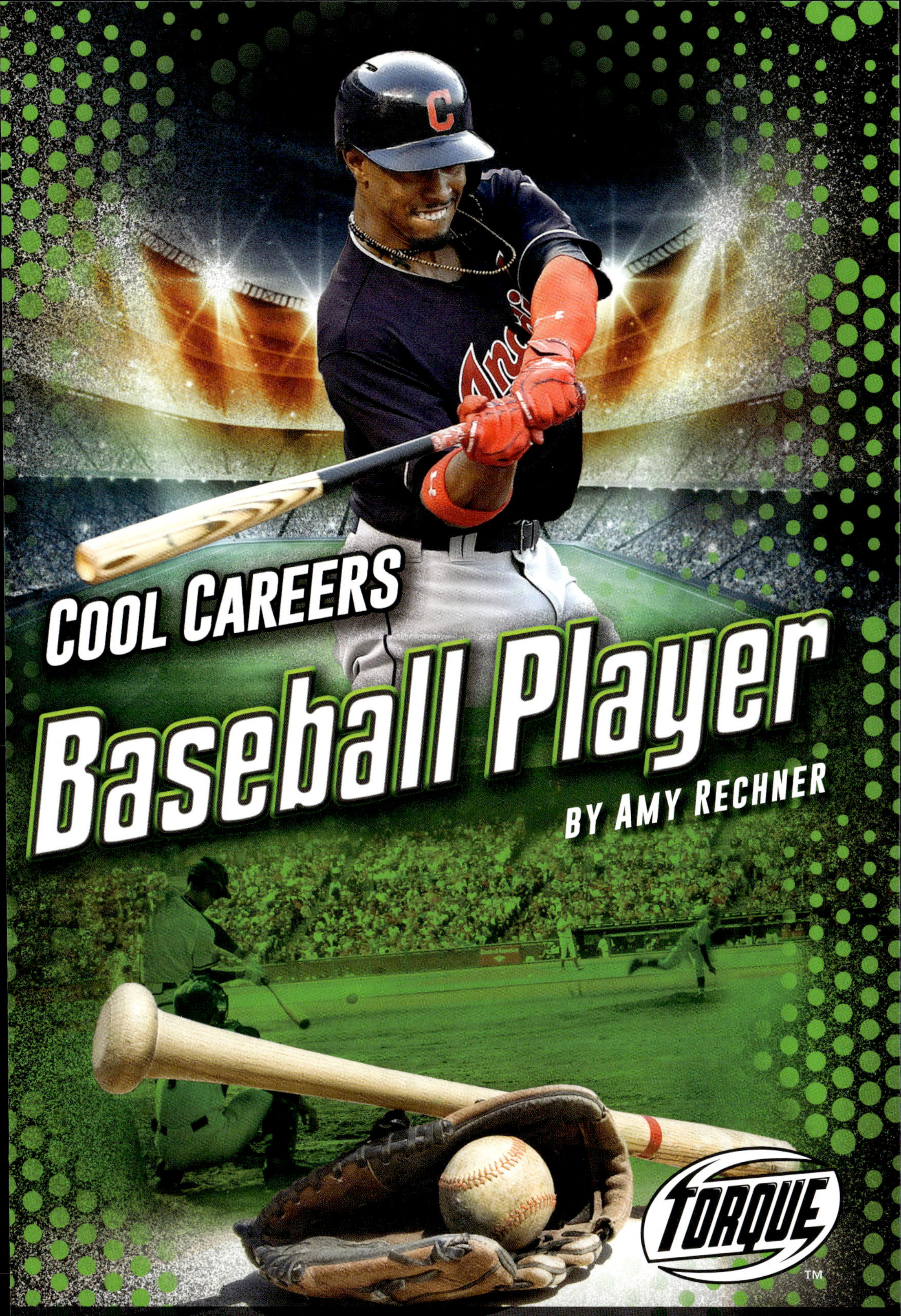

COOL CAREERS

Baseball Player

BY AMY RECHNER

BELLWETHER MEDIA • MINNEAPOLIS, MN

TORQUE™

Are you ready to take it to the extreme? Torque books thrust you into the action-packed world of sports, vehicles, mystery, and adventure. These books may include dirt, smoke, fire, and dangerous stunts.
WARNING: read at your own risk.

This edition first published in 2020 by Bellwether Media, Inc.

Library of Congress Cataloging-in-Publication Data

Names: Rechner, Amy, author.
Title: Baseball Player / by Amy Rechner.
Description: Minneapolis, MN : Bellwether Media, Inc., 2020. | Series: Torque. Cool Careers | Includes bibliographical references and index. | Audience: Grade 3 to 7.
Identifiers: LCCN 2018061023 (print) | LCCN 2019007327 (ebook) | ISBN 9781618916280 (ebook) | ISBN 9781644870617 (hardcover : alk. paper)
Subjects: LCSH: Baseball–Juvenile literature. | Baseball players–Juvenile literature.
Classification: LCC GV867.5 (ebook) | LCC GV867.5 .R425 2020 (print) | DDC 796.357–dc23
LC record available at https://lccn.loc.gov/2018061023

Editor: Kate Moening   Designer: Josh Brink

Printed in the United States of America, North Mankato, MN.

TABLE OF CONTENTS

Batter Up!

The score is tied after eight **innings**. The **relief pitcher** warms up his arm. He is known as the closer. He will pitch the ninth inning.

The pitcher runs out to the mound. He feels strong. He throws fastballs to strike out three batters. Then his team is up to bat. Crack! A home run! They win!

FAST BALL

Pitchers throw most balls at around 90 miles (145 kilometers) per hour! This is very hard on players' arms. Relief pitchers come in so players do not hurt themselves.

In the Big Leagues

Kids play in baseball and softball leagues all through school. Many dream of **careers** in the **major league**. Major league players play in front of huge crowds of fans!

Most **professional** baseball players are in the **minor league**. They may spend years working their way to the top of the game.

Eri Yoshida

A GAME FOR EVERYONE

Women can play professional baseball too, but no women have played for a major league team yet. Japanese pitcher Eri Yoshida played for the Chico Outlaws for two seasons!

Arizona training camp

A baseball player's year begins with spring training, which starts in January or February. Teams practice in warm places like Arizona or Florida.

Players work on their **fielding** and batting skills. They work out to build muscles and **endurance**. Trainers help them overcome or avoid injury. Some minor league players are invited to train with major league teams.

Famous Face

Javier (Javy) Báez

POSITION PLAYED: CHICAGO CUBS SECOND BASEMAN, SHORTSTOP, AND THIRD BASEMAN

BORN: DECEMBER 1, 1992

HOMETOWN: BAYAMÓN, PUERTO RICO

EDUCATION: HIGH SCHOOL (ARLINGTON COUNTRY DAY SCHOOL)

PREVIOUS EXPERIENCE: HIGH SCHOOL BASEBALL; THREE YEARS OF MINOR LEAGUE BASEBALL

ACHIEVEMENTS:

- NATIONAL LEAGUE CHAMPIONSHIP SERIES CO-MOST VALUABLE PLAYER (MVP), 2016
- STARTING SECOND BASEMAN, 2018 ALL-STAR GAME
- NICKNAMED "EL MAGO" (THE MAGICIAN) BECAUSE HE PLAYS SO MANY POSITIONS WELL

Javier Báez

The baseball season usually begins in April. Sometimes the weather is still wintry. Wet grass and cold winds create challenges for ballplayers.

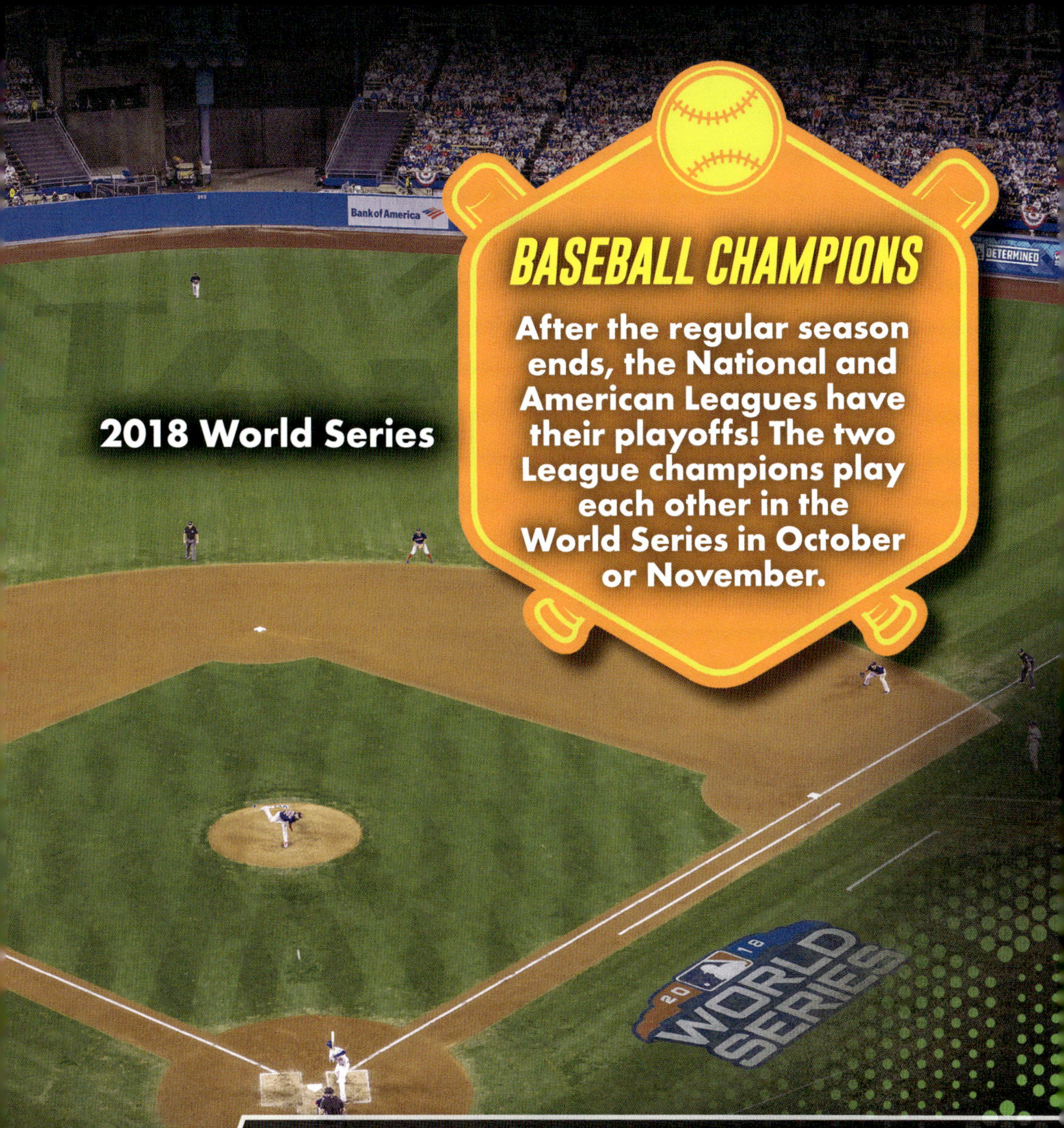

2018 World Series

BASEBALL CHAMPIONS

After the regular season ends, the National and American Leagues have their playoffs! The two League champions play each other in the World Series in October or November.

Teams play 162 games in 187 days from March or April to September. They travel and play in all weather. After the season is over, players rest and take care of injuries. Playing baseball is a tough job!

Team Players

warming up to bat

Players arrive at the ballpark several hours before the first pitch. They stretch and work out with trainers at the team clubhouse. Warm-ups include batting and catching on the field.

When the game starts, batters grab their helmets and gloves and head to the plate! Catchers wait behind them. They wear thick face masks and padding to stay safe.

WHAT IS IN A BAT?

Major league baseball bats must be made of wood! There are many different kinds, but the teams make sure a player always has their favorite.

Players who are fielding run to guard the bases and outfield. With their leather mitts, they are ready to catch anything!

stretching

After a long game, players take time to stretch and take baths. This helps their bodies stay healthy. Then they leave for the next series of games in another city!

During the season, a baseball team is like a family. Players spend most of their time with their teammates. They must work closely and get along. There is also a large coaching staff for the team.

Trainers help the players with exercising and injuries. They make sure the players are healthy and able to play.

Game Day Checklist

☑ **2:00 PM:** WORK OUT: WEIGHTLIFTING, STRETCHING, AND DRILLS

☑ **2:30 PM:** SOAK AND REST MUSCLES

☑ **3:00 PM:** BATTING PRACTICE

☑ **3:30 PM:** LUNCH

☑ **4:30 PM:** WARM-UP: STRETCHING, RUNNING, FIELDING

☑ **5:15 PM:** BREAK TIME: RELAX, SNACK, WATCH TV, PLAY VIDEO GAMES

☑ **6:15 PM:** DRESS FOR THE GAME; MORE STRETCHING AND WARM-UPS

☑ **7:00 PM:** GAME ON!

Road to the Majors

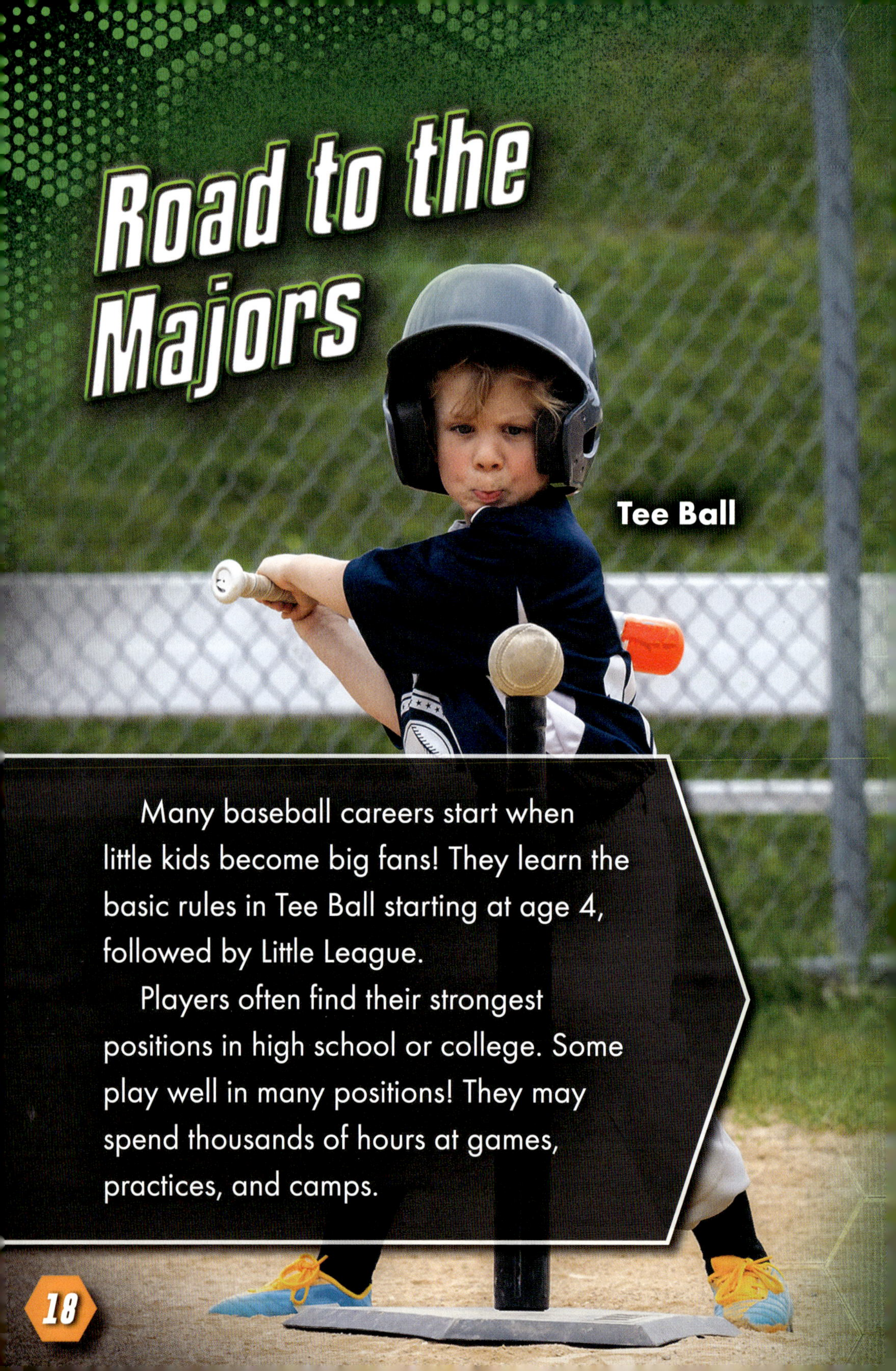

Tee Ball

Many baseball careers start when little kids become big fans! They learn the basic rules in Tee Ball starting at age 4, followed by Little League.

Players often find their strongest positions in high school or college. Some play well in many positions! They may spend thousands of hours at games, practices, and camps.

Career Path

LITTLE LEAGUE

HIGH SCHOOL / COLLEGE BASEBALL

MINOR LEAGUES

MAJOR LEAGUES

FRIENDLY FACES

One skill all players need is good manners! Being friendly to fans and polite to reporters is all part of a professional ballplayer's job.

Baseball **scouts** attend high school, college, and **independent league** games. They find players to try out for major league **clubs**. Once they are picked for a club, **rookies** often play for the club's minor league teams. One day they may join the majors!

Not every player makes it to the major leagues. But they all share a lifelong love of the game!

Baseball Player Wanted!

LOOKING FOR BASEBALL PLAYERS, ALL POSITIONS: FUTURE MAJOR LEAGUE CAREER A POSSIBILITY

EDUCATION: HIGH SCHOOL DIPLOMA; SOME COLLEGE A PLUS

EXPERIENCE: LITTLE LEAGUE, YOUTH LEAGUES, HIGH SCHOOL AND COLLEGE TEAMS

QUALITIES:
- TEAM PLAYER
- FAST SPRINTER
- STRONG HITTER
- WILLING TO TRAVEL

SALARIES FOR MAJOR LEAGUE POSITIONS CAN REACH MORE THAN $30,000,000!

Glossary

careers—jobs that people do for a long time

clubs—major league baseball teams and the minor league teams each one is connected to

endurance—the ability to do something difficult for a long time

fielding—catching and throwing balls

independent league—a professional baseball group that is not part of a major league club

innings—parts of a baseball game; there are nine innings in a regular game.

major league—the highest-ranking league of American professional baseball; major league teams usually get their players from minor league teams.

minor league—professional baseball leagues that compete at lower levels than the major leagues; the minor leagues are divided into six skill levels.

professional—a person who makes money playing baseball

relief pitcher—a baseball pitcher who takes over for another pitcher during the game

rookies—first-year players in a professional sport

scouts—people whose job is to find talented new players for major league clubs

To Learn More

AT THE LIBRARY

Braun, Eric. *Pro Baseball's Underdogs: Players and Teams Who Shocked the Baseball World.* North Mankato, Minn.: Capstone Press, 2018.

Pina, Andrew. *Becoming a Pro Baseball Player.* New York, N.Y.: Gareth Stevens Publishing, 2015.

Velasco, Catherine Ann. *Behind the Scenes of Pro Baseball.* North Mankato, Minn.: Capstone Press, 2019.

ON THE WEB

FACTSURFER

Factsurfer.com gives you a safe, fun way to find more information.

1. Go to www.factsurfer.com.
2. Enter "baseball player" into the search box and click .
3. Select your book cover to see a list of related web sites.

Index

The images in this book are reproduced through the courtesy of: Tribune Content Agency LLC/ Alamy, front cover (hero), p. 9; joebelanger, front cover (equipment); Richard Paul Kane, pp. 4, 5; fstop123, p. 6; JoeSAPhotos, p. 7; STR/ Stringer/ Getty Images, p. 7 (Eri Yoshida); Aflo Co. Ltd./ Alamy, p. 8; Scott W. Grau/ AP Images, p. 10; Joseph Saum, p. 11; Cal Sport Media/ Alamy, p. 12; Scott Lomenzo, p. 13; Aspen Photo, pp. 14, 19 (top right); Jeff Roberson/ AP Images, p. 15; Ira Berger/ Alamy, p. 16; Jeff Smith, p. 17 (top); Flavio Beltran, p. 17 (top middle); Carlos E. Santa Maria, p. 17 (bottom middle); Paul Yates, p. 17 (bottom); Jonathan Novack, p. 18; gyro, p. 19 (top left); Bill Florence, p. 19 (bottom left); Keeton Gale, pp. 19 (bottom right), 20; Keeton10, p. 21.